Canterbury guide 2025

Uncover Timeless Charm, Hidden Alleys, and 21st-Century Surprises in England's Historic Gem

Kieroksen Sage

@2025 Kieroksen Sage

All rights reserved.

No part of this book may be reproduced, stored in a retrieval system, or transmitted in any form or by any means—electronic, mechanical, photocopying, recording, or otherwise—without prior written permission from the publisher or author, except for brief quotations used in reviews or articles.

Table of contents

Table of contents 2
Chapter 1: Welcome to Canterbury 8
   1.1 Why Canterbury in 2025? A Journey Through Centuries 8
      A Landmark Anniversary 8
      Medieval Meets Modern 9
      Sustainable Soul 10
   1.2 Beyond the Cathedral: Art, Culture, and Riverside Magic 11
      A Canvas of Creativity 11
      Riverside Reverie 12
      Cultural Crossroads 12
   1.3 Canterbury at a Glance: A Snapshot of the City's Soul 13
      Neighborhoods in Miniature 13
      Local Flavors 14
      The Canterbury Vibe 15
     Why You'll Fall in Love 16
Chapter 2: Planning Your Pilgrimage 17
   2.1 Before You Go 17
   1.1 Best Times to Visit: Seasonal Festivals & Quiet Escapes 17
      1.2 Budget Tips: Affordable Stays, Free Attractions & Local Deals 20
   1.3 Sustainable Travel: Eco-Friendly Practices in 2025 22
   2.2 Getting Here & Around 23

2.1 Airports, Trains, and Scenic Road Trips 24

2.2 Public Transport Made Easy: Buses, Bikes, and Walking Routes 25

2.3 Navigating Like a Local: Parking Hacks and Pedestrian Zones 26

Why This Plan Works 27

Chapter 3: Exploring Canterbury 29

3.1 Must-See Sights 29

1.1 Iconic Landmarks: Canterbury Cathedral, St. Augustine's Abbey, Westgate Towers 29

1.2 2025 Highlights: Newly Restored St. Martin's Church & River Stour Boardwalk 32

1.3 Hidden Gems: Secret Gardens, Tudor Alleys, and Ghostly Tales 33

3.2 Neighborhood Vibes 34

2.1 The Cathedral Quarter: Cobblestones and Timeless Elegance 34

2.2 King's Mile: Boutiques, Bookshops, and Artisan Eats 35

2.3 Canterbury Riverside: Pubs, Parks, and Modern Cafés 36

3.3 Family-Friendly Fun 37

3.1 Canterbury Tales Immersive Experience: 2025 Interactive Upgrades 38

3.2 Howletts Wild Animal Park: New Safari Lodges and Conservation Talks 38

3.3 Westgate Gardens: Picnics, Puppet Shows, and Medieval Reenactments 39

Why Canterbury Captivates 40

Chapter 4: History Unearthed 42

4.1 Canterbury's Living Past 42

1.1 The Pilgrims' Path: Chaucer's Legacy and Modern-Day Quests..42

1.2 Roman Canterbury: Ruins, Museums, and the Ancient City Wall..43

1.3 WWII Heritage: Secret Tunnels and Blitz Stories 44

4.2 Museums & Galleries..45

2.1 The Beaney House of Art & Knowledge: 2025 Exhibits 46

2.2 Canterbury Roman Museum: Hands-On Archaeology for Kids..47

2.3 Sidney Cooper Gallery: Contemporary Art in a Victorian Setting..48

Why Canterbury's History Resonates 49

chapter 5: Flavors of Canterbury 50

5.1 Culinary Delights...51

1.1 Classic Canterbury: Kentish Rarebit, Canterbury Tart, and Ale 51

1.2 2025 Food Trends: Farm-to-Table Pioneers and Vegan Feasts..53

1.3 Food Markets: Goods Shed and Canterbury Farmers' Market..54

5.2 Pubs, Tea Rooms & Cafés 55

2.1 Historic Pubs: The Old Weavers House and The Parrot..55

2.2 Coffee Culture: Specialty Roasters and Riverside Brews..57

2.3 Afternoon Tea: Best Scones with Cathedral Views 58

Conclusion 59

Chapter 6: Day Trips from Canterbury 61

    6.1 Coastal Escapes 61

        1.1 Whitstable: Oysters, Art Galleries, and Beach Huts 62

        1.2 Dover: White Cliffs, Castle Secrets, and 2025 Viking Exhibits 64

    6.2 Historic Havens 65

        2.1 Leeds Castle: Jousting Festivals and Lavender Fields 65

        2.2 Rochester: Dickensian Streets and Cathedral Treasures 67

    Conclusion 69

Chapter 7: Need-to-Know Essentials 71

    7.1 Stay Connected 71

        1.1 Free Wi-Fi Spots and Tech-Friendly Spaces 71

        1.2 Visitor Centers and Helpful Apps 73

    7.2 Safety & Accessibility 74

        2.1 Emergency Contacts and Health Resources 74

        2.2 Wheelchair-Friendly Attractions and Accommodations 76

    7.3 Local Etiquette 77

        3.1 Canterbury Customs: Politeness, Tipping, and Pub Culture 77

        3.2 Supporting Small Businesses in 2025 78

    Conclusion 80

Chapter 8: Farewell for Now 82

    8.1 Take a Piece of Canterbury Home 82

        1.1 Souvenirs with Soul: Local Crafts, Books, and Kentish Wines 83

- 1.2 Share Your Story: #Canterbury2025 85
- 8.2 See You Soon 86
  - 2.1 Reasons to Return: Unfinished Adventures 86
  - 2.2 Canterbury's Vision for 2030 and Beyond .. 88
- Conclusion: A Goodbye, but Not Forever 90

Appendices 91
- 9.1 Canterbury Neighborhood Map with Key Landmarks 91
  - Historic City Centre 92
  - St. Dunstan's & West Canterbury 93
  - Northgate & St. Radigund's 93
  - St. Martin's & The Outer East 93
  - South Canterbury & Wincheap 94
- 9.2 2025 Event Calendar (Month-by-Month Highlights) 94
  - January – New Beginnings & Winter Wonders . 95
  - February – Romance & Heritage 95
  - March – Cultural Awakening 96
  - April – Easter Festivities 96
  - May – Outdoor Adventures 96
  - June – Summer Festivities 97
  - July – Arts & Music Extravaganza 97
  - August – Outdoor Leisure & Heritage Tours 97
  - September – Literature & Learning 98
  - October – Autumnal Festivities 98
  - November – Remembrance & Reflection 99
  - December – Christmas in Canterbury 99
- 9.3 Local Lingo Guide (e.g., "Pilgrim," "Drovers," "Kentish Hug") 99

  Pilgrim 100
  Drovers 100
  Kentish Hug 100
  Westgate Wander 101
  Ale Trail 101
  The Chaucer Shuffle 101
Conclusion 102

Chapter 1: Welcome to Canterbury

Where Ancient Stones Whisper and Modern Creativity Thrives

1.1 Why Canterbury in 2025? A Journey Through Centuries

Canterbury isn't just a destination—it's a time capsule. In 2025, this medieval marvel celebrates its layered history while embracing a future brimming with innovation. Here's why this year is the perfect moment to explore England's spiritual heart:

A Landmark Anniversary

2025 marks the **850th anniversary of Thomas Becket's martyrdom** at Canterbury Cathedral, a pivotal moment that transformed the city into Europe's most revered pilgrimage site. To honor this legacy, the cathedral unveils Lighting the Way, a year-long program featuring illuminated manuscript exhibits, choral performances of 12th-century Gregorian chants, and twilight torchlit tours tracing Becket's final steps. Don't miss the **Pilgrim's Progress Festival** (July 12–20), where costumed storytellers, falconry displays, and artisan markets revive the spirit of Chaucer's Canterbury Tales.

Medieval Meets Modern

Canterbury's 2025 skyline harmonizes ancient spires with contemporary creativity. The newly restored **St. Martin's Church** (Britain's oldest parish church) debuts a **virtual reality time portal**, letting visitors "walk" through 1,400 years of history, from Saxon baptisms to Tudor upheavals. Meanwhile, the **River Stour Boardwalk**, completed in spring 2025, adds a sleek, accessible pathway linking the cathedral to the **Canterbury Riverside Innovation Hub**—a repurposed Victorian tannery now housing indie galleries and eco-conscious startups.

Sustainable Soul

Canterbury leads Kent's green revolution. The 2025 **Zero Carbon Pilgrimage** initiative encourages travelers to offset their journey via tree-planting in Blean Woods (a medieval forest turned rewilding project). Stay at **The Sun Hotel**, a 15th-century coaching inn now powered by geothermal energy, or join a **plastic-free punting tour** along the Stour, where guides trade disposable cups for reusable flasks of locally pressed apple juice.

1.2 Beyond the Cathedral: Art, Culture, and Riverside Magic

While the cathedral dominates postcards, Canterbury's true magic lies in its lesser-known corners—places where art, nature, and community collide.

A Canvas of Creativity

- **The Beaney House of Art & Knowledge**: This 2025 exhibit, Rebels & Romantics, showcases Kentish artists who defied convention, from Victorian feminist painter Joanna Boys to punk collage collective Rogue Gene. Free workshops let you screen print protest posters or craft Tudor-style love letters.
- **Sidney Cooper Gallery**: A 19th-century barn turned avant-garde space. Summer 2025 features Threads of Time, a textile

installation weaving Canterbury's wool trade history with AI-generated tapestries.
- **Graffiti Alley (St. Peter's Lane)**: A rotating open-air gallery where street artists reimagine Chaucer's pilgrims as cyborgs and steampunk heroes.

Riverside Reverie

The River Stour isn't just a backdrop—it's the city's lifeline. Glide past weeping willows on a **guided punt** (2025's electric boats are whisper-quiet) or rent a kayak from **Canterbury Punting Company** to explore hidden channels where kingfishers dart. For a romantic twist, book the **Supper Under the Stars** package: a three-course meal on a candlelit punt, paired with Kentish wines and live harp music.

Cultural Crossroads

- **Marlowe Theatre:** Named for Canterbury's Elizabethan playwright, this venue's 2025 lineup includes a punk-rock Macbeth and a Canterbury Tales ballet scored by electronic duo Massive Attack.
- **Westgate Towers**: Climb England's largest surviving medieval gatehouse for rooftop views, then descend into its new **Undercroft Jazz Bar**, where saxophonists riff under 600-year-old stone arches.

1.3 Canterbury at a Glance: A Snapshot of the City's Soul

Canterbury's charm lies in its contradictions—a place where cloistered monks once chanted, and today's students debate philosophy over craft beer. Here's how to capture its essence:

Neighborhoods in Miniature

- **The Cathedral Quarter**: Cobblestone streets lined with timber-framed houses. Pop into **The Chaucer Bookshop** for first editions, then sip espresso at **Tiny Tim's Tearoom** beneath crooked oak beams.
- **King's Mile**: A pedestrianized haven of indie shops. Hunt for truffle oil at **The Goods Shed** market or bespoke leather journals at **The Shakespeare's Head**.
- **Canterbury Riverside**: A revitalized district where Victorian warehouses now host microbreweries like **The Foundry**, which infuses porter with foraged elderflower.

Local Flavors

Canterbury's cuisine mirrors its history—hearty, inventive, and deeply rooted:
- **Kentish Rarebit**: The 2025 twist at **Deeson's British Restaurant** adds ale-

soaked figs and Canterbury Cobble cheese.

- **Canterbury Tart**: A medieval recipe revived at **The Ambrette** with saffron-poached pears and clotted cream.
- **Pork & Co.**: Nose-to-tail dining in a converted chapel. Try the "Becket's Feast"—slow-roasted pork belly with mead glaze.

The Canterbury Vibe

- **Slow Travel**: Rent a **Brompton bike** (£10/day) to pedal the Crab & Winkle Trail, a 7-mile route through orchards and Norman churches.
- **Community Spirit**: Join the **Canterbury Commons** volunteer group (Saturdays, 9 AM) to plant wildflowers along the city walls.

- **Festive Energy**: From the **Canterbury Festival** (October's arts bonanza) to the **Dickensian Christmas Market** (mulled wine and carolers in cloisters), the city thrives on celebration.

Why You'll Fall in Love

Canterbury in 2025 isn't frozen in time—it's alive. It's the thrill of tracing your fingers over Saxon stonework, then debating AI ethics with university students at a riverside pub. It's the warmth of a baker handing you a still-wheaty "pilgrim's loaf" fresh from the oven, and the quiet awe of standing in a cathedral that's weathered plagues, wars, and pilgrims' prayers for nearly a millennium.

Come for the history. Stay for the stories that are still being written.

Chapter 2: Planning Your Pilgrimage

Your Blueprint for a Seamless, Savvy, and Soulful Canterbury Journey

2.1 Before You Go

Canterbury rewards travelers who plan with intention. Whether you're chasing cherry blossoms in spring or cozying up in a medieval tavern in winter, a little preparation ensures you'll savor every moment—without overspending or overlooking the city's green heart.

1.1 Best Times to Visit: Seasonal Festivals & Quiet Escapes

Canterbury's seasons each tell a different story. Here's how to align your trip with the city's rhythm:

Spring (March–May)
- **Why Visit**: Blossoming orchards, mild weather, and the **Canterbury Festival of Blooms** (April 5–13, 2025), where floral installations transform the cathedral cloisters into a fragrant wonderland.
- **Quiet Tip**: Visit in late March to avoid Easter crowds. Stroll the **Westgate Gardens** as daffodils bloom, or join a dawn chorus walk in **Blean Woods** with local birders.

Summer (June–August)
- **Highlights**: The **Pilgrim's Progress Festival** (July 12–20) revives Chaucer's tales with jousting, mead tastings, and street performers.

- **Beat the Crowds**: Arrive at the cathedral by 8:30 AM to admire stained glass in peace. Book a **sunset punt tour** on the Stour for golden-hour views of the city walls.

Autumn (September–November)
- **Local Secret**: September's **Canterbury Food & Drink Fair** (Sept 20–22) pairs Kentish wines with foraging workshops in the countryside.
- **Serenity**: October's misty mornings are ideal for photography. Capture the cathedral spire shrouded in fog, then warm up with spiced apple cider at **The Moat Tea Rooms**.

Winter (December–February)
- **Magic**: The **Dickensian Christmas Market** (Dec 1–23) fills Buttermarket Square with carolers, mulled wine, and handcrafted gifts.

- **Budget Perk**: January's **"Winter Warmers"** hotel deals include free entry to the Canterbury Roman Museum and discounted three-course meals at **Deeson's British Restaurant.**

1.2 Budget Tips: Affordable Stays, Free Attractions & Local Deals

Canterbury delivers old-world charm without draining your wallet:

Sleep Smart

- **Hostels with History: Kipps' Canterbury** (a converted Victorian schoolhouse) offers dorm beds from £25/night, including a Kentish breakfast.
- **B&Bs**: **The Millers Arms** (£65/night) serves homemade marmalade and grants free access to their riverside sauna.

Free & Fabulous

- **Canterbury Cathedral Grounds**: While the cathedral interior costs £16, the Precincts (gardens and cloisters) are free to explore.
- **City Walls Walk**: Follow the 2-mile medieval wall for panoramic views. Download the **Canterbury Histories** app for free audio tales of siege engines and smuggler tunnels.
- **The Beaney House**: Free entry to its eclectic art collection and quirky exhibits like "Roman Board Games Night" (first Fridays).

2025 Discounts

- **Canterbury Passport**: New in 2025! For £45, get entry to 3 attractions (cathedral, Roman Museum, Westgate Towers) + a £10 food voucher.

- **Student Perks:** Flash a university ID for 20% off punting tours and £5 tickets to Marlowe Theatre matinees.

1.3 Sustainable Travel: Eco-Friendly Practices in 2025

Canterbury leads Kent's green revolution. Here's how to tread lightly:

Stay Green

- **The Sun Hotel:** A 15th-century inn now carbon-neutral, with rooftop solar panels and toiletries in refillable ceramic jars.
- **Canterbury Eco Camp:** Glamping pods (£55/night) made from recycled ship timber, nestled in an apple orchard.

Explore Responsibly

- **Bike Shares:** Rent e-bikes via **Canterbury Cycle Co-op** (£10/day). Follow the **Crab & Winkle Trail** to

Whitstable, a car-free route through bluebell woods.
- **Plastic-Free Punting: Canterbury Punting Company** swaps single-use cups for engraved copper mugs (keep yours as a souvenir).

Give Back
- **Zero Carbon Pilgrimage**: Offset your trip by planting oak saplings in **Blean Woods** (£5/tree). Receive GPS coordinates to visit "your" tree in future years.
- **Litter Patrols**: Join the **Green Pilgrims** group (Saturdays, 9 AM) for a cleanup walk along the Stour, rewarded with free coffee at **Waterstones Café**.

2.2 Getting Here & Around

Canterbury's compact size and revamped 2025 transit make arrival effortless—and exploring a joy.

2.1 Airports, Trains, and Scenic Road Trips

By Air

- **London Gatwick (LGW)**: 1.5 hours by train. Take the **Gatwick Express** to London Bridge, then transfer to Southeastern Rail.
- **London Stansted (STN)**: 2 hours via National Express coach (direct to Canterbury Bus Station).

By Train

- **High Speed from London St Pancras**: 53 minutes to Canterbury West Station. Book advance tickets for £15–£25.

- **Scenic Coastal Route**: From Dover Priory (20 minutes), pass white cliffs and WWII bunkers.

By Car
- **A2 Road Trip**: Detour through the **Kent Downs** (Area of Outstanding Natural Beauty). Stop at **Chilham Village** for a pub lunch at **The White Horse**, a 14th-century haunt.
- **EV Charging**: Free ports at **Longport Car Park** and **Whitefriars Shopping Centre**.

2.2 Public Transport Made Easy: Buses, Bikes, and Walking Routes

Buses
- **UniBus U1**: Links Canterbury East Station to the University of Kent (£2.50 single). Runs every 10 minutes.

- **Stagecoach Triangle**: Circular route connecting cathedral, hospital, and supermarkets (£1.50/day pass).

Bikes
- **Brompton Hire**: Foldable bikes (£10/day) available at Canterbury West Station. Use the **Cycling Canterbury** app for traffic-free routes.

Walking
- **Pedestrian Zones**: The city center (High Street, Guildhall Street) is car-free 10 AM–6 PM. Follow the **Red Pavement Arrows** for a self-guided heritage walk.

2.3 Navigating Like a Local: Parking Hacks and Pedestrian Zones

Parking Secrets

- **Longport Car Park**: £6/day, 5 minutes from the cathedral. Pre-book via **JustPark** for £4.50.
- **Free Sundays**: On-street parking is free citywide on Sundays.

Avoid Traffic

- **Rush Hour**: Steer clear of St George's Roundabout 8–9 AM and 5–6 PM. Use **New Dover Road** as a bypass.

Local Lingo

- "Drovers": Slang for Canterbury's bus drivers. A friendly "Cheers, drover!" earns smiles.
- "Kentish Hug": A hearty handshake—expect it at B&Bs and pubs.

Why This Plan Works

Canterbury in 2025 is a city that welcomes you with open arms—and well-marked footpaths. Whether you're sipping cider in a sun-dappled orchard or tracing the footsteps of medieval pilgrims, every detail here is designed to make your pilgrimage effortless and unforgettable. Pack your curiosity (and a reusable water bottle), and let Canterbury surprise you.

Chapter 3: Exploring Canterbury

Uncover Layers of History, Vibrant Communities, and Family Adventures

3.1 Must-See Sights

Canterbury's landmarks are more than postcard backdrops—they're living stories. From awe-inspiring cathedrals to tucked-away treasures, these sights reveal the city's soul.

1.1 Iconic Landmarks: Canterbury Cathedral, St. Augustine's Abbey, Westgate Towers

Canterbury Cathedral
A UNESCO World Heritage Site and spiritual

heart of England, this Gothic masterpiece has drawn pilgrims since 597 AD. In 2025, don't miss:

- **The Martyrdom Chapel**: Stand where Thomas Becket was slain in 1170. New augmented reality tablets overlay holograms of medieval pilgrims praying at his shrine.
- **Chapter House**: Marvel at 13th-century stained glass restored in 2025 using medieval techniques. Join the **Whispering Walls Tour** (Sundays, £10) to hear acoustic secrets—a single voice can carry across the 90-foot vaulted hall.
- **Bell Harry Tower**: Climb 176 steps for panoramic views. Time your ascent for noon to hear the **2025 Jubilee Bell** ring, cast to honor the cathedral's anniversary.

St. Augustine's Abbey

These haunting ruins mark where Christianity

began in England. The 2025 **Monastic Life Experience** lets you:
- Script Latin manuscripts with quills in the Scriptorium.
- Taste 6th-century monk's stew (barley, leeks, and wild herbs) at pop-up **Abbey Kitchen** events.

Westgate Towers

England's largest surviving medieval gatehouse now doubles as a museum and viewpoint. New for 2025:
- **Timekeeper's Challenge**: Solve clockmaker puzzles in the 14th-century turret to unlock a rooftop champagne toast.
- **Undercroft Jazz Bar**: Sip Kentish gin beneath 600-year-old arches during Friday night live sessions.

1.2 2025 Highlights: Newly Restored St. Martin's Church & River Stour Boardwalk

St. Martin's Church
Britain's oldest parish church (built in 597 AD) reopens in April 2025 after a £2 million restoration:

- **Virtual Time Portal:** Wear VR headsets to witness Queen Bertha's baptism and Saxon-era weddings.
- **Silent Garden:** A new contemplative space with stone benches carved from original Roman-era masonry.

River Stour Boardwalk
This £1.5 million elevated pathway (completed June 2025) links the cathedral to Canterbury Riverside:

- **Eco-Art Installations**: Solar-powered lanterns shaped like medieval fishing traps light the route at night.
- **Otter Watch Points**: Binocular stations spot the river's resurgent otter population.

1.3 Hidden Gems: Secret Gardens, Tudor Alleys, and Ghostly Tales

Greyfriars Chapel & Gardens
A Franciscan friary-turned-secret garden. Follow the **Chaucer's Birds Trail** (free map) to spot goldcrests and nuthatches among 14th-century arches.

The Crooked House of King's Mile
This 17th-century leaning timber shop (17 Palace Street) sells rare books on alchemy. Ask owner Martha to share tales of its rumored witch trials connection.

Ghost Walks
- **Canterbury Ghost Tours**: Friday nights at Westgate Towers (£12). "Meet" plague victims and executed smugglers in the old prison cells.
- **Lady Wootton's Green**: Locals swear that Tudor square's benches are warmed by the ghost of a wool merchant's wife.

3.2 Neighborhood Vibes

Canterbury's neighborhoods are like siblings—each with distinct personalities but bound by shared history.

2.1 The Cathedral Quarter: Cobblestones and Timeless Elegance

Must-Visits:
- **The Chaucer Bookshop**: First editions and handwritten poetry in a 15th-century weaver's cottage.

- **Tiny Tim's Tearoom**: Order the "Becket Blend" tea with saffron scones beneath sagging oak beams.
- **Canterbury Historic River Tours**: Electric punts (£18pp) glide past medieval wash houses now converted into artist studios.

2025 Tip: Every Saturday morning, local cheesemongers set up stalls in the Butter Market. Try the award-winning **Canterbury Cobble**—a nutty, ash-rinded cheese.

2.2 King's Mile: Boutiques, Bookshops, and Artisan Eats

Shopping Highlights:
- **The Goods Shed**: A Victorian train station turned food hall. Grab Kentish oysters at **The Fish Counter** or truffle oil at **The Truffleist**.

- **The Shakespeare's Head**: Quill pens and handmade leather journals in a shop haunted by the ghost of a 16th-century playwright (so they say).

Foodie Finds:
- **The Veg Box Café**: Vegan "fish" and chips made with banana blossom, served in a converted horse stable.
- **The Foundry Brewpub**: Try the **Pilgrim's Porter** aged in bourbon barrels from Canterbury's twin city, Louisville, Kentucky.

2.3 Canterbury Riverside: Pubs, Parks, and Modern Cafés

Riverside Pubs:
- **The Old Weavers House**: 16th-century haunt with a secret tunnel (now a wine cellar). Order the **Weaver's Pie**—beef,

ale, and mashed potato under a pastry loom.
- **The Parrot**: Claims to be England's oldest pub (1189 AD). Their 2025 **Time Traveler's Tasting Menu** pairs medieval mead with molecular gastronomy.

Green Spaces:
- **Tannery Field**: A new 2025 riverside park with hammock groves and free outdoor yoga (Saturdays, 9 AM).
- **Pocket Gardens**: Miniature fairy gardens hidden in nooks along High Street—snap photos for #CanterburyMagic.

3.3 Family-Friendly Fun

Canterbury delights visitors of all ages with adventures that educate, thrill, and inspire.

3.1 Canterbury Tales Immersive Experience: 2025 Interactive Upgrades

This attraction inside a medieval church now features:

- **AI Chaucer**: A holographic guide who adapts stories based on kids' questions. ("What did knights really eat?")
- **Smell-O-Vision**: Scratch-and-sniff cards release scents of medieval markets (spices, hay, and… less pleasant aromas).
- **Knight Training**: Kids don replica armor to "joust" with foam lances in the cloisters.

3.2 Howletts Wild Animal Park: New Safari Lodges and Conservation Talks

2025 Additions:

- **Rhino Retreat Lodges**: Sleep in elevated pods overlooking the African plains exhibit. Night vision goggles provided.
- **Keeper Kids**: A 2-hour program where children 8+ prepare food for lemurs and track animal footprints.

Pro Tip: Visit at 2 PM for the **Elephant Splash Zone**, where rescued Asian elephants cool off—prepare to get wet!

3.3 Westgate Gardens: Picnics, Puppet Shows, and Medieval Reenactments

Family Activities:
- **Storybook Sundays**: Costumed actors perform The Canterbury Tales as puppet shows (free, 11 AM weekly).

- **Dragon Quest**: A scavenger hunt to find 10 stone dragons hidden in the gardens (prize: a golden chocolate coin).
- **Tudor Picnic Kits**: Rent wicker baskets (£15) filled with honey-roasted ham, elderflower cordial, and a checkerboard for lawn games.

Why Canterbury Captivates

Canterbury isn't about ticking off sights—it's about stepping into a storybook where every cobblestone has a tale. It's the thrill of hearing your echo bounce through a 1,400-year-old crypt, the joy of watching your child's face light up as a holographic Chaucer cracks jokes, and the peace of sipping cider in a sunlit orchard that's fruited since Saxon times. Whether you're here for three days or three weeks, let Canterbury surprise you. After all, the best adventures begin with a curious heart and sturdy walking shoes.

Chapter 4: History Unearthed

Where Ancient Footsteps Echo and Modern Stories Begin

4.1 Canterbury's Living Past

Canterbury's history isn't confined to textbooks—it pulses through its cobblestone streets, whispers in its cloisters, and surfaces in unexpected corners. Here, every era leaves a mark, inviting you to walk in the footsteps of pilgrims, Romans, and wartime heroes.

1.1 The Pilgrims' Path: Chaucer's Legacy and Modern-Day Quests

Chaucer's Canterbury Tales comes alive in 2025, blending medieval lore with contemporary adventures. Start at the

Canterbury Tales Immersive Experience, where holographic storytellers recount The Miller's Tale amid smells of hay and ale (scratch-and-sniff cards included!). For a tangible pilgrimage, follow the **Pilgrims' Way**, a 13-mile trail from Winchester to Canterbury, revitalized in 2025 with new waymarkers and rest stops. Modern pilgrims can earn a **Digital Pilgrim Badge** by scanning QR codes at key sites like **St. Thomas's Hospital Ruins**, where medieval travelers sought healing.

2025 Highlight: Join the **Chaucer Festival** (October 12–19), featuring costumed parades, mead tastings, and a "Best Middle English Limerick" contest judged by local historians.

1.2 Roman Canterbury: Ruins, Museums, and the Ancient City Wall

Beneath Canterbury's medieval veneer lies its Roman soul. The **Canterbury Roman Museum** sits atop a 1st-century townhouse, its mosaic floors preserved under glass walkways. New for 2025:

- **Digventures**: Kids excavate replica Roman artifacts in a mock archaeological pit (free with admission).
- **Lights of Durovernum**: Evening tours project augmented reality scenes of Roman markets onto the ruins.

Don't miss the **Roman City Wall Trail**, a 2-mile walk along Britain's oldest surviving fortifications. Pause at **Queningate**, a "haunted" gatehouse where locals swear they've heard centurions' ghostly drills.

Pro Tip: Pair your Roman exploration with lunch at **Café Roma**, dishing up sourdough panis and honeyed figs near the museum.

1.3 WWII Heritage: Secret Tunnels and Blitz Stories

Canterbury's WWII legacy is etched in its scars and survival. Explore:

- **The Canterbury Blitz Experience**: A 2025 interactive exhibit in the **Marlowe Theatre basement**, where vibrations and soundscapes recreate the 1942 air raids. Survivors' audio testimonies play as you navigate a blackout maze.
- **Secret Tunnels**: Beneath **St. Augustine's Abbey**, newly opened tunnels reveal wartime shelters carved by monks. Guides share tales of hidden art treasures and midnight resistance meetings.

Local Hero: Visit **Lady Wootton's Green**, where a plaque honors firewatcher Elsie Knocker, who saved dozens during the Blitz. Her great-granddaughter leads monthly storytelling walks (£10, includes wartime rations tasting).

4.2 Museums & Galleries

Canterbury's museums aren't just repositories of the past—they're dynamic spaces where history shakes hands with innovation.

2.1 The Beaney House of Art & Knowledge: 2025 Exhibits

This eclectic museum marries art, anthropology, and oddities. 2025's must-sees:

- **Rebels of the Isles**: A Kentish focus on suffragette Alice Zimmern and punk artist Linder Sterling. Interactive displays let you design protest posters or remix punk anthems.
- **Cabinet of Curiosities**: A new wing showcasing "Canterbury's Forgotten Eccentrics," including a Victorian cat taxidermist and a 1920s time-travel hoaxer.

Freebie: Every Thursday, join **Tea & Theory** sessions—sip Kentish lavender tea while curators debate art's role in climate activism.

2.2 Canterbury Roman Museum: Hands-On Archaeology for Kids

More than mosaics, this museum engages young explorers:

- **Roman Detective Trail**: Solve clues to find a "stolen" artifact, winning a laurel wreath selfie filter.
- **Dress Like a Durovernum Citizen**: Toga rentals and face-painting stations (gladiator scars optional).

2025 Update: The **Mosaic Workshop** lets families craft tile replicas using Roman techniques (£15, bookings essential).

2.3 Sidney Cooper Gallery: Contemporary Art in a Victorian Setting

Housed in a 19th-century barn, this gallery juxtaposes heritage with avant-garde:

- **Threads of Time** (May–Sept 2025): Textile artist Nnenna Okore weaves Canterbury's wool trade history into suspended installations using recycled fishing nets from Kent's coast.
- **AI Ancestors**: A digital exhibit where visitors upload selfies to see their faces reimagined as Roman settlers or Saxon farmers.

Local Secret: The gallery's hidden **Courtyard Studio** hosts free life-drawing classes every Sunday, with models posing as historical figures (Henry VIII optional).

Why Canterbury's History Resonates

Canterbury doesn't just display history—it invites you to live it. It's tracing your finger over a Roman mosaic, then sipping espresso in a café built atop a medieval inn. It's laughing as your child dons a centurion's helmet, and shivering as a Blitz survivor's story echoes in a candlelit tunnel. In 2025, the city bridges past and present with wit, warmth, and a dash of rebellion. Whether you're a history buff, a curious wanderer, or a family seeking adventure, Canterbury's layers await your discovery.

chapter 5: Flavors of Canterbury

Canterbury is a city of history, culture, and timeless charm, but it's culinary scene is just as rich and diverse. From traditional dishes rooted in Kent's agricultural heritage to contemporary food trends that embrace sustainability and innovation, the city offers a feast for all tastes. Whether you are indulging in a warm Canterbury Tart, enjoying a pint in a historic pub, or sipping artisanal coffee by the riverside, the flavors of Canterbury create a lasting impression. This chapter delves into the culinary treasures of Canterbury, highlighting classic dishes, emerging food trends, bustling markets, and the inviting ambiance of its pubs, tea rooms, and cafés.

5.1 Culinary Delights

1.1 Classic Canterbury: Kentish Rarebit, Canterbury Tart, and Ale

Canterbury's culinary traditions are deeply rooted in the local produce and farming practices of Kent, often referred to as "the Garden of England." The region's fertile soil and favorable climate make it an ideal location for growing fruits, vegetables, and hops, contributing to its vibrant food scene.

One of Canterbury's most celebrated dishes is **Kentish Rarebit**, a variation of the classic Welsh rarebit. This dish consists of a thick slice of bread topped with a rich cheese sauce made from locally produced Kentish cheese, ale, and mustard. The combination of flavors is both comforting and satisfying, making it a popular choice among visitors and locals alike.

Another beloved Canterbury specialty is the **Canterbury Tart**, a delicious dessert that captures the essence of Kent's fruit-growing heritage. Made with a crisp pastry crust and a filling of tangy lemon curd, it is often garnished with apples or cherries, which are abundant in the region. This tart embodies the perfect balance of sweetness and tartness, making it a delightful end to any meal.

No exploration of Canterbury's flavors would be complete without mentioning its **traditional ales**. Canterbury's brewing history dates back centuries, with local breweries crafting exceptional ales using Kentish hops. Many pubs and restaurants proudly serve locally brewed pints, ensuring that visitors can experience the authentic taste of Canterbury's beer culture.

1.2 2025 Food Trends: Farm-to-Table Pioneers and Vegan Feasts

The city is also embracing modern food movements, particularly the **farm-to-table** ethos. Canterbury's proximity to local farms means that restaurants can source fresh ingredients directly from growers, ensuring high-quality, seasonal dishes. Many eateries are championing this approach, offering menus that change with the seasons and celebrate regional produce.

Alongside farm-to-table dining, **vegan and plant-based cuisine** is becoming increasingly popular in Canterbury. More restaurants and cafés are offering innovative plant-based options that appeal to vegans, vegetarians, and even meat-eaters seeking healthier and more sustainable meals. Dishes such as beetroot tartare, jackfruit tacos, and dairy-free desserts showcase the city's commitment to catering to diverse dietary preferences.

1.3 Food Markets: Goods Shed and Canterbury Farmers' Market

For those who prefer a more interactive culinary experience, Canterbury's food markets are a must-visit.

The Goods Shed, a renowned food hall and market, is an institution in the city. Operating as both a farmers' market and a restaurant, it offers an array of fresh produce, artisan cheeses, locally baked bread, and organic meats. The market's commitment to sustainability and quality makes it a favorite among food lovers who appreciate knowing where their food comes from.

Another notable market is the **Canterbury Farmers' Market**, where local producers sell everything from handmade jams and chutneys to free-range eggs and organic vegetables. The market is a hub for those looking to connect with the region's farmers and food artisans while discovering the best Canterbury has to offer.

5.2 Pubs, Tea Rooms & Cafés

2.1 Historic Pubs: The Old Weavers House and The Parrot

Canterbury's pubs are more than just places to enjoy a drink—they are steeped in history, each with a story to tell.

The Old Weavers House, situated along the River Stour, dates back to the 16th century and offers visitors a glimpse into Canterbury's past. With its timber-framed structure and stunning river views, it provides the perfect setting to enjoy a traditional meal accompanied by a pint of local ale. The menu often features hearty British classics like steak and ale pie, fish and chips, and Sunday roasts.

Another iconic establishment is **The Parrot**, one of Canterbury's oldest pubs, housed in a medieval building with origins tracing back to the 14th century. With its rustic wooden beams and cozy atmosphere, The Parrot serves a selection of local craft beers and an excellent gastropub menu that showcases the best of Kent's ingredients. From locally sourced lamb dishes to hand-battered fish, this pub is a favorite among those seeking an authentic taste of Canterbury.

2.2 Coffee Culture: Specialty Roasters and Riverside Brews

Canterbury's coffee scene has evolved significantly in recent years, with a growing number of independent coffee shops and specialty roasters setting new standards for quality and craftsmanship.

One standout café is **Lost Sheep Coffee**, which has built a reputation for its exceptional single-origin beans and expertly crafted espresso drinks. Sourcing its beans directly from farmers and roasting them locally, Lost Sheep Coffee embodies the dedication to quality that defines Canterbury's coffee culture.

For those who enjoy a scenic coffee experience, several cafés along the River Stour offer **riverside brews** where patrons can enjoy their drinks while watching the tranquil waters flow by. Whether it's a hand-poured V60 or a creamy flat white, Canterbury's coffee scene has something to please every caffeine enthusiast.

2.3 Afternoon Tea: Best Scones with Cathedral Views

A visit to Canterbury wouldn't be complete without indulging in a **traditional afternoon tea**. The city boasts several tea rooms that offer a refined yet comforting experience, complete with freshly baked scones, clotted cream, and fragrant loose-leaf teas.

One of the best spots for afternoon tea is **Tiny Tim's Tearoom**, a charming establishment known for its vintage décor and impeccable service. Here, guests can savor classic English tea alongside homemade cakes and scones, all served on elegant tiered stands.

For those who wish to enjoy their tea with a stunning view, some tea rooms near **Canterbury Cathedral** provide a breathtaking backdrop. Sipping a cup of Earl Grey while gazing at the cathedral's Gothic spires is an experience that combines culinary delight with historical grandeur.

Conclusion

The flavors of Canterbury tell a story—one of history, innovation, and deep appreciation for quality food and drink. Whether you are relishing a classic Kentish dish, exploring modern food trends, or enjoying a drink in a centuries-old pub, Canterbury offers a feast for both the palate and the soul. With its rich culinary heritage and exciting new dining experiences, the city ensures that every visitor leaves with not only fond memories but also a satisfied appetite. For food lovers and adventurers alike, Canterbury is a destination that continues to inspire and delight.

Chapter 6: Day Trips from Canterbury

Canterbury is a city rich in history and charm, but its surroundings offer equally captivating experiences. A short journey from the city will lead you to breathtaking coastal towns, magnificent castles, and historic havens brimming with cultural treasures. Whether you seek the salty breeze of the seaside, the intrigue of medieval strongholds, or the charm of literary landmarks, the region around Canterbury is packed with unforgettable day-trip destinations. This chapter explores some of the best excursions from Canterbury, ensuring that visitors make the most of their time in Kent and beyond.

6.1 Coastal Escapes

1.1 Whitstable: Oysters, Art Galleries, and Beach Huts

Just a short 20-minute drive or train ride from Canterbury, **Whitstable** is a picturesque seaside town known for its maritime heritage, thriving arts scene, and world-famous oysters. A visit here offers a perfect blend of relaxation and exploration.

Oysters & Seafood: Whitstable's oyster farming tradition dates back to Roman times, making the town synonymous with this delicacy. The **Whitstable Oyster Company** is a must-visit for those wanting to indulge in fresh, locally harvested oysters, while seafood lovers will also appreciate the variety of restaurants serving everything from grilled lobster to traditional fish and chips. The annual **Whitstable Oyster Festival** in the summer celebrates this culinary heritage with live music, street food, and traditional boat parades.

Art & Culture: Beyond its culinary delights, Whitstable is home to a thriving artistic community. The **Fishslab Gallery** and **Gallery 64a** showcase contemporary works from local and emerging artists, while **The Horsebridge Arts Centre** hosts exhibitions, workshops, and live performances. Strolling through Whitstable, visitors will also find independent boutiques selling handcrafted jewelry, ceramics, and unique home decor.

Beachfront & Nature: A walk along the **Tankerton Slopes** offers stunning sea views and a chance to admire the town's colorful beach huts. These charming wooden structures are iconic symbols of Whitstable's seaside charm. For those looking to explore the coastline further, a beach walk toward

Seasalter or a sailing trip in the bay provides a serene way to experience the beauty of the Kentish coast.

1.2 Dover: White Cliffs, Castle Secrets, and 2025 Viking Exhibits

A half-hour journey from Canterbury, **Dover** is famous for its dramatic white cliffs, rich history, and bustling port. A visit to this town offers a mix of natural beauty and fascinating history.

The White Cliffs of Dover: One of the most recognizable natural landmarks in Britain, the **White Cliffs of Dover** provide breathtaking views over the English Channel. Visitors can hike along the cliff-top trails, taking in the fresh sea air while spotting rare birds and wildflowers. The cliffs have long been a symbol of Britain's resilience and were historically the first sight for returning travelers and soldiers.

Dover Castle: Perched atop the cliffs, **Dover Castle** is a medieval fortress with over 900 years of history. Known as the "Key to England," the castle has played a crucial role in defending Britain from invasions. Visitors can explore the Great Tower, where King Henry II once entertained guests, and venture into the secret wartime tunnels used during World War II.

2025 Viking Exhibits: History buffs will be especially excited about the **Viking Exhibit**, debuting in 2025. This new addition showcases artifacts, interactive displays, and immersive reconstructions of Viking life in Dover, highlighting the town's connections to these seafaring warriors.

6.2 Historic Havens

2.1 Leeds Castle: Jousting Festivals and Lavender Fields

A 45-minute drive from Canterbury brings visitors to one of the most stunning castles in England, **Leeds Castle**. Surrounded by a serene moat, rolling parklands, and beautifully manicured gardens, the castle is a must-see for history lovers and families alike.

The Castle & Its Legacy: Originally built in the 12th century, Leeds Castle has served as a Norman stronghold, a royal residence for six medieval queens, and even a retreat for Henry VIII. Today, it is a well-preserved historical site offering guided tours through its opulent interiors, complete with tapestries, grand halls, and period furnishings.

Jousting & Events: A major highlight of Leeds Castle is its annual **Jousting Festival**, where knights in shining armor compete in dramatic tournaments on horseback. This event transports visitors back in time to the age of chivalry, complete with medieval music, falconry displays, and costumed performers.

Gardens & Lavender Fields: Beyond the castle, visitors can wander through the breathtaking **Culpeper Garden**, the **Woodland Walk**, and the fragrant **lavender fields**, which bloom beautifully in summer. The castle's grounds also feature a maze, an underground grotto, and a serene lake, making it an ideal destination for a full day of exploration.

2.2 Rochester: Dickensian Streets and Cathedral Treasures

For a literary and historical journey, **Rochester** is an exceptional destination. Just under an hour from Canterbury, this charming town is closely associated with Charles Dickens and boasts an array of historical landmarks.

Dickensian Heritage: Rochester was a great source of inspiration for Charles Dickens, who spent part of his life here and featured the town in many of his novels. Fans of the famed author can visit **The Guildhall Museum**, which contains exhibitions on Dickens and his characters, as well as the **Six Poor Travellers' House**, a setting in one of his short stories. The annual **Dickens Festival** in June brings the streets to life with costumed characters, performances, and Victorian-themed festivities.

Rochester Cathedral & Castle: The town is also home to **Rochester Cathedral**, one of England's oldest and most beautiful cathedrals, dating back to the 7th century. Visitors can admire its stunning Norman architecture, intricate stained-glass windows, and the ancient crypt. Just a short walk away, **Rochester Castle** stands as one of the best-preserved Norman castles in the country. Climbing its towering keep rewards visitors with panoramic views over the River Medway.

Quaint Streets & Independent Shops: Rochester's **High Street** is a delightful blend of history and modern charm. Lined with antique bookstores, boutique shops, and cozy cafés, it's the perfect place to stroll, shop, and enjoy a leisurely afternoon tea. Whether browsing for rare books or sampling homemade fudge, visitors will find plenty of hidden gems.

Conclusion

Canterbury's surroundings are as enchanting as the city itself, offering visitors a diverse range of day-trip experiences. Whether you're indulging in fresh seafood by the sea, exploring ancient castles, or stepping into the pages of Dickens' novels, the region provides countless opportunities for adventure. These destinations capture the heart of England's rich heritage and natural beauty, ensuring that every trip from Canterbury is an unforgettable journey into the past and present.

Chapter 7: Need-to-Know Essentials

Visiting Canterbury is a delightful experience, but being well-prepared can make your journey even more enjoyable. Whether you're staying for a weekend or an extended stay, understanding key aspects of connectivity, safety, accessibility, and local customs can enhance your time in the city. This chapter provides practical insights into staying connected, ensuring safety and accessibility, and embracing Canterbury's cultural etiquette to help you navigate the city seamlessly.

7.1 Stay Connected

1.1 Free Wi-Fi Spots and Tech-Friendly Spaces

Staying connected while exploring Canterbury is essential for navigating the city, sharing experiences, or catching up on work. Thankfully, the city offers a variety of **free Wi-Fi spots** and **tech-friendly spaces** to keep visitors online.

Public Wi-Fi Locations: Many popular areas in Canterbury provide free Wi-Fi, including **Whitefriars Shopping Centre**, **Canterbury Cathedral Precincts**, and the **Westgate Gardens**. Additionally, most cafes, such as **The Beaney House of Art & Knowledge** and **Kitch Café**, offer complimentary internet access to customers.

Libraries and Co-Working Spaces: If you need a quiet place to work or study, Canterbury's public library, **The Beaney**, offers free Wi-Fi, comfortable seating, and printing facilities. There are also co-working spaces like **Fruitworks**, which cater to digital nomads, freelancers, and business travelers looking for a productive environment.

1.2 Visitor Centers and Helpful Apps

Canterbury Visitor Information Centre, located near the Cathedral Gate, is a great first stop for travelers. Here, visitors can access maps, brochures, and expert advice on attractions, events, and public transport.

For tech-savvy travelers, various **helpful apps** can make navigation and planning easier:

- **Google Maps & Citymapper** – For real-time public transport routes and walking directions.
- **Canterbury Park & Ride** – Helps with parking options and shuttle bus schedules.

- **Visit Canterbury App** – Provides recommendations on attractions, food, and upcoming events.
- **Trainline & National Rail** – Essential for checking train schedules to and from Canterbury.
- **Uber & Local Taxi Apps** – Ensure easy transportation when needed.

7.2 Safety & Accessibility

2.1 Emergency Contacts and Health Resources

Understanding emergency contacts and health resources can provide peace of mind while visiting Canterbury.

Emergency Numbers:

- **999** – For police, fire, and medical emergencies.
- **111** – For non-urgent medical advice.
- **Canterbury Police Station:** Old Dover Road, Canterbury CT1 3JQ.
- **Kent & Canterbury Hospital:** Located at Ethelbert Road, Canterbury, this is the main hospital for urgent medical assistance.

For minor ailments, **local pharmacies** like **Boots Pharmacy (High Street)** provide over-the-counter medicines and health consultations.

Travel Insurance & Medical Clinics: If you need non-emergency medical care, walk-in clinics such as **Canterbury Health Centre** can assist visitors. Travelers are encouraged to have **travel insurance** to cover unexpected medical costs.

2.2 Wheelchair-Friendly Attractions and Accommodations

Canterbury is increasingly becoming more **accessible to visitors with disabilities**. Many attractions, public transport services, and accommodations have taken steps to ensure ease of mobility.

Wheelchair-Friendly Attractions:

- **Canterbury Cathedral** – While parts of the historic cathedral have steps, ramps and accessible entrances are available. The visitor center also provides wheelchairs on request.
- **The Beaney House of Art & Knowledge** – Fully accessible with lifts and designated seating areas.
- **Westgate Gardens** – A beautiful, flat landscape that is easy to navigate.

- **The Marlowe Theatre** – Offers step-free access and special seating for visitors with mobility needs.

Transport & Accommodation: Most buses in Canterbury are equipped with **low floors** and designated wheelchair spaces. Additionally, many hotels, such as **ABode Canterbury** and **Premier Inn**, offer accessible rooms with adapted bathrooms and step-free entry.

7.3 Local Etiquette

3.1 Canterbury Customs: Politeness, Tipping, and Pub Culture

Visitors to Canterbury will find that **politeness and courtesy** are integral to British culture. Saying "please," "thank you," and "excuse me" goes a long way when interacting with locals.

Tipping Culture: While tipping is not compulsory, it is appreciated. In restaurants, a **10-12.5% service charge** is often included in the bill. If it's not, a tip of around **10%** is customary for good service. In pubs, tipping is not expected, but a friendly "thank you" to the bartender is always welcomed.

Pub Etiquette: Canterbury's pub culture is a cherished experience. When ordering drinks at the bar, it's customary to pay immediately rather than running a tab. If someone buys you a drink, it's polite to **return the favor** later in the evening. Many traditional pubs also have beer gardens, perfect for enjoying a pint outdoors.

3.2 Supporting Small Businesses in 2025

Canterbury thrives on its independent shops, family-run eateries, and artisan markets.

Supporting local businesses enhances your experience and helps sustain the city's unique character.

Where to Shop & Eat Local:

- **Goods Shed** – A fantastic farmers' market with fresh local produce, cheeses, and meats.
- **Canterbury Farmers' Market** – Showcases homemade preserves, crafts, and seasonal goods.
- **Independent Bookstores** – Such as **The Chaucer Bookshop**, perfect for literary lovers.
- **Local Cafés & Restaurants** – Try **Oscar & Bentleys** for a cozy meal or **The Skinny Kitchen** for fresh, health-conscious options.

Eco-Friendly Shopping & Dining: Many small businesses in Canterbury emphasize sustainability. Visitors can shop at **zero-waste stores** and dine at restaurants offering organic and locally sourced ingredients. Choosing these establishments helps support Canterbury's commitment to a greener future.

Conclusion

Being well-prepared with the right information enhances any trip to Canterbury. From staying connected with free Wi-Fi and helpful apps to ensuring safety through emergency contacts and accessible facilities, these essentials contribute to a stress-free visit. Understanding local customs, such as tipping and pub etiquette, also enriches your cultural experience. Most importantly, supporting small businesses ensures that Canterbury's unique charm continues to thrive for years to come. By keeping these essentials in mind, visitors can fully immerse themselves in the city's history, hospitality, and vibrant community.

Chapter 8: Farewell for Now

Visiting Canterbury is more than just a journey through history, culture, and breathtaking landscapes—it is an experience that stays with you long after you leave. From the echoing chimes of the cathedral bells to the charm of its cobbled streets, this city has a way of making visitors feel at home. While your time here may be coming to an end, there are countless ways to take a piece of Canterbury with you, ensuring that your connection to this enchanting city endures. This chapter highlights how you can carry the spirit of Canterbury with you, share your experiences, and find compelling reasons to return.

8.1 Take a Piece of Canterbury Home

1.1 Souvenirs with Soul: Local Crafts, Books, and Kentish Wines

Bringing home a meaningful souvenir is one of the best ways to keep your Canterbury memories alive. Rather than settling for generic mementos, explore the city's unique and locally crafted treasures that reflect its history, artistry, and charm.

Local Crafts & Artisanal Goods: Canterbury has a thriving community of artisans producing everything from handmade jewelry to traditional pottery. The **Canterbury Makers** collective, found in various pop-up locations and markets, showcases beautifully crafted goods made by local artists. For something truly special, visit **Conquest House Gallery**, which features paintings, sculptures, and crafts that capture the essence of Canterbury's rich heritage.

Literary Keepsakes: As a city deeply intertwined with literary history, Canterbury offers an array of books that make for perfect souvenirs. A visit to **The Chaucer Bookshop** or **Waterstones Canterbury** provides an opportunity to pick up classic and contemporary works related to the city. Whether it's a copy of The Canterbury Tales or a modern novel set in the area, these books serve as a reminder of your journey through this literary landscape.

Kentish Wines & Gourmet Treats: The region surrounding Canterbury is home to some of England's finest vineyards. Bringing back a bottle of **Kentish wine**, such as those from **Chapel Down** or **Biddenden Vineyards**, allows you to savor the flavors of Canterbury long after you leave. Additionally, locally produced **Canterbury honey, Kentish ale, and**

handmade chocolates make for excellent gifts or personal treats that encapsulate the city's rich culinary heritage.

1.2 Share Your Story: #Canterbury2025

In today's digital world, sharing travel experiences has never been easier—or more rewarding. By posting your favorite Canterbury moments online using **#Canterbury2025**, you not only preserve your memories but also inspire future travelers to explore this historic city.

Capture the Best Moments: Whether it's a sunset view from the **Westgate Gardens**, a hidden gem found in the city's side streets, or a memorable meal at a cozy café, sharing these experiences allows others to see Canterbury through your eyes.

Engage with the Canterbury Community: The city has a welcoming and engaged online presence. By tagging local businesses, visitor centers, and cultural organizations, you contribute to Canterbury's storytelling and support the community.

Reflect on Your Journey: Writing about your trip—whether in a blog, travel journal, or even a simple social media post—helps to cement the experience in your memory. Describe what surprised you, what moved you, and what left you wanting more. These reflections will serve as a reminder of why Canterbury holds a special place in your heart.

8.2 See You Soon

2.1 Reasons to Return: Unfinished Adventures

One of the best things about Canterbury is that no matter how much time you spend here, there is always more to discover. Whether it's a hidden corner of the city, an annual festival, or an experience you didn't get to try, there are countless reasons to return.

Seasonal Events & Festivals: Canterbury's events calendar is packed with celebrations that transform the city throughout the year. Perhaps your next visit will coincide with the **Canterbury Festival**, the city's biggest arts and culture event, or the festive **Christmas Market**, where the city lights up with holiday charm.

Unexplored Landmarks: Did you get the chance to explore all of Canterbury's historic sites? Maybe your next visit will include a guided tour of the lesser-known medieval ruins or a deeper dive into the city's Roman history at the **Canterbury Roman Museum**.

A New Culinary Experience: The food scene in Canterbury is always evolving. With new restaurants, cafés, and pop-up markets emerging, each visit presents an opportunity to indulge in something new and exciting. Whether you missed out on trying a famous Kentish dish or want to explore the latest farm-to-table trends, the city's food culture will always have something fresh to offer.

2.2 Canterbury's Vision for 2030 and Beyond

Canterbury is not just a city steeped in history—it is a place that is always looking forward. As it continues to grow and evolve, there are exciting plans for the future that will make future visits even more rewarding.

Sustainable Tourism & Green Initiatives: The city is committed to becoming a leader in sustainable tourism. With initiatives such as increasing pedestrian-friendly zones, enhancing green spaces, and promoting eco-friendly businesses, Canterbury aims to create a **greener and more environmentally responsible** destination by 2030.

Cultural & Architectural Developments: As Canterbury continues to invest in its arts and culture scene, visitors can expect to see new museum exhibitions, performance spaces, and historical restorations that make each return trip feel like a new adventure.

Enhanced Visitor Experiences: The city is working on improving accessibility and visitor services, making it even easier for travelers to explore Canterbury's treasures. From updated digital guides to new interactive exhibits, Canterbury's tourism experience is set to become even more engaging.

Conclusion: A Goodbye, but Not Forever

Saying farewell to Canterbury is never truly a goodbye—it's more of a "see you later." Whether you leave with a handcrafted souvenir, a collection of stunning photographs, or a heart full of cherished memories, Canterbury will always be waiting for your return.

As the city moves forward into the future, so too does the promise of new discoveries, experiences, and adventures. Until then, may the stories of Canterbury continue to inspire you, and may your memories of this remarkable city always bring a smile to your face.

So, until we meet again—**farewell for now, and see you soon in Canterbury!**

Appendices

The journey through Canterbury is enriched not only by its stunning landmarks and historic depth but also by its local nuances, seasonal vibrancy, and unique cultural expressions. The following appendices provide visitors with an easy reference for navigating the city, staying informed about key events, and embracing the charming local lingo. Whether you're a first-time traveler or a returning visitor, these resources will help you experience Canterbury more deeply and authentically.

9.1 Canterbury Neighborhood Map with Key Landmarks

Understanding the layout of Canterbury is crucial for making the most of your visit. The city is compact and walkable, with distinct neighborhoods offering unique experiences. Below is a brief guide to some of the most notable areas and their key attractions.

Historic City Centre

- Canterbury Cathedral – The heart of the city and a UNESCO World Heritage Site, this awe-inspiring structure has been welcoming pilgrims for centuries.
- The King's Mile – A collection of charming, independent shops, cafes, and historic pubs.
- The Marlowe Theatre – A hub for entertainment, offering world-class performances year-round.
- Westgate Towers & Gardens – The city's medieval entrance and a peaceful riverside retreat.

St. Dunstan's & West Canterbury

- St. Dunstan's Church – The final resting place of Thomas More's head, with a history dating back to Saxon times.
- Westgate Parks – Ideal for a tranquil walk along the River Stour.

Northgate & St. Radigund's

- Canterbury Christ Church University – A lively area filled with students and local cafes.
- St. Radigund's Street – A hidden gem lined with traditional homes and historic sites.

St. Martin's & The Outer East

- St. Martin's Church – The oldest continuously used church in England.

- Canterbury Roman Museum – A fascinating journey into the city's ancient past.

South Canterbury & Wincheap

- Canterbury East Railway Station – A key transport hub connecting the city to London and beyond.
- Dane John Gardens – A lovely green space perfect for a picnic or leisurely stroll.

With these key landmarks in mind, navigating Canterbury becomes an effortless and enjoyable experience.

9.2 2025 Event Calendar (Month-by-Month Highlights)

Canterbury is a city of festivals, traditions, and celebrations. Below is a month-by-month breakdown of some of the most anticipated events in 2025.

January – New Beginnings & Winter Wonders

- New Year's Fireworks at Westgate Gardens – A breathtaking display to welcome the year.
- Canterbury Winter Market – A perfect spot for cozy winter shopping and local delicacies.

February – Romance & Heritage

- Valentine's River Tours – Special boat rides on the Stour for couples.
- Canterbury Literary Festival – Celebrating local and international authors.

March – Cultural Awakening

- St. Patrick's Day Pub Crawl – A festive way to explore the city's best historic pubs.
- Spring Equinox Celebration at St. Augustine's Abbey – Marking the arrival of spring with heritage walks and storytelling.

April – Easter Festivities

- Canterbury Easter Fair – A traditional fair with local crafts and entertainment.
- Historic Walking Tours – Focused on Canterbury's medieval and Roman past.

May – Outdoor Adventures

- Canterbury May Day Festival – Traditional music, dancing, and flower festivals.

- Westgate Gardens Spring Picnic Series – Free outdoor concerts and food markets.

June – Summer Festivities

- Midsummer Tudor Banquet – A reenactment dining experience at The Parrot.
- Canterbury Food & Drink Festival – A paradise for foodies featuring Kentish specialties.

July – Arts & Music Extravaganza

- Canterbury Music Festival – Live performances across different venues in the city.
- Medieval Pageantry at the Cathedral – Costumed reenactments and historical storytelling.

August – Outdoor Leisure & Heritage Tours

- Pilgrims' Trail Guided Walk – A retracing of the famous Canterbury pilgrimage route.
- Open-Air Cinema at Dane John Gardens – Classic films under the summer sky.

September – Literature & Learning

- The Chaucer Festival – Celebrating The Canterbury Tales with performances and talks.
- University Welcome Weeks – Cultural activities open to the public at Canterbury's universities.

October – Autumnal Festivities

- Canterbury Festival – A two-week arts and culture celebration.
- Ghost Walks & Haunted Canterbury – Spooky stories from the city's eerie past.

November – Remembrance & Reflection

- Bonfire Night at Westgate Gardens – Fireworks and traditional treats.
- Remembrance Sunday Service at the Cathedral – Honoring history and heritage.

December – Christmas in Canterbury

- Canterbury Christmas Market – A festive fair filled with crafts, food, and seasonal joy.
- Candlelit Carols at the Cathedral – A magical way to celebrate the season.

9.3 Local Lingo Guide (e.g., "Pilgrim," "Drovers," "Kentish Hug")

Every city has its own unique set of words and phrases, and Canterbury is no exception. Here's a guide to some of the local lingo that might come in handy during your visit.

Pilgrim

Refers to the historic travelers who journeyed to Canterbury to visit the shrine of St. Thomas Becket. Even today, many visitors refer to themselves as "modern pilgrims" when making the trek to the cathedral.

Drovers

Historically, these were livestock herders who moved sheep and cattle across Kent. Some of Canterbury's streets and routes were once old driving paths, now filled with quaint shops and markets.

Kentish Hug

A friendly greeting often used in Canterbury and surrounding areas. While not as widely known outside Kent, it embodies the warm and welcoming spirit of the region.

Westgate Wander

A phrase locals use to describe a leisurely stroll along the scenic Westgate Gardens and River Stour.

Ale Trail

A popular phrase used to describe a self-guided journey through Canterbury's best historic pubs, sampling locally brewed ales along the way.

The Chaucer Shuffle

A lighthearted term referring to the slow and often meandering way tourists explore the city's cobbled streets while following The Canterbury Tales-themed walking routes.

Conclusion

These appendices serve as a valuable resource for exploring Canterbury with confidence and curiosity. Whether you're mapping out the best landmarks, planning your visit around key events, or picking up a few local phrases to impress the residents, this guide ensures that you leave Canterbury with a richer, deeper connection to the city.

As Canterbury continues to evolve while preserving its historic charm, we hope this guide serves as a reminder that there is always something new to discover—whether on your first visit or your tenth.

So go forth, explore, and embrace all that Canterbury has to offer!

Printed in Great Britain
by Amazon